FUN
WITH
WASHI

35 Ways to Instantly Refresh Your Home,
Accessories, and Packages with Washi Tape

. . . .

JESSICA OKUI

photographs by ANGIE CAO

CHRONICLE BOOKS
SAN FRANCISCO

Text and illustrations copyright © 2014 by Jessica Okui.

Photographs copyright © 2014 by Angie Cao.

Library of Congress Cataloging-in-Publication Data:
Okui, Jessica.
  Fun with washi : 35 ways to instantly refresh your home, accessories, and packages with washi tape / Jessica Okui.
    pages cm
  ISBN 978-1-4521-2919-8
1. Tape craft. 2. Gummed paper tape. 3. Masking tape.
4. Japanese paper. I. Title.

  TT869.7.O47 2014
  736'.980952—dc23

                    2013040459

Manufactured in China

Designed by Cat Grishaver

10 9 8 7 6 5 4 3 2 1

Chronicle Books LLC
680 Second Street
San Francisco, California 94107
www.chroniclebooks.com

ACKNOWLEDGMENTS

Fun with Washi could not have been created without the support, encouragement, and love of many important people past and present in my life. Thank you to:

Lisa Tauber from Chronicle Books who guided and supported me throughout the creation of this book.

. . . .

Mrs. Ann Thorpe, my high school graphic design teacher, who encouraged me to pursue a degree in the arts.

. . . .

Ms. Janice Golojuch, my college graphic design instructor and mentor, who inspired me.

. . . .

My grandmothers, Barbara Roehl and Ruth Spring, who would always have craft projects for me when I visited them.

. . . .

Above all, I am thankful for my loving husband, Jason, who has supported and believed in me from the very beginning. Also my children, Evan and Morgan, who inspire me with their creativity.

CONTENTS

HOME DÉCOR

ACCESSORIES *and* EMBELLISHMENTS

STATIONERY *and* PACKAGING

INTRODUCTION

Welcome to the wonderful, versatile world of washi tape. Washi is a traditional Japanese-style paper made out of natural materials such as bark, bamboo, and rice. When combined with masking tape, washi paper becomes the beloved craft material washi tape, also known to some as Japanese masking tape, paper tape, or tissue tape.

Washi tape is similar to traditional masking tape in that it's a low-tack tape that's easy to remove from most surfaces, but it's thinner, more flexible, and has a smoother texture.

Washi tape comes in a wonderful array of unique colors and prints—perfect for all sorts of craft projects. You can use the tape on a variety of materials, from paper to glass to fabric, to add color and sophisticated accents to your home, your stationery, and even your clothing. And washi tape is easily removed and repositioned, so you can change up your décor whenever you want, but the tape will stay in place until you remove it.

When I discovered washi tape, I instantly fell in love with the medium. I had never seen anything quite like it. Unlike most types of artist tape, it has a translucent quality that adds a unique look to craft projects. I also like the organic character of it; you can just rip the tape instead of cutting it with scissors and it still looks nice. Washi tape has

inspired me to think of new and exciting ways to add details to everything around me, many of which you'll find in the thirty-five projects in this book. Embellish a wall with removable wallpaper, cut the tape into tiny pieces to make mosaic coasters, iron it onto fabric to add a bold print to your tote, or wrap up your gifts with a distinctive bow. Since washi tape is so simple to use, the projects are easy to make no matter your skill level. In fact, all of the projects can be created in less than an hour, some in a matter of minutes, and many only require basic materials like scissors and glue—perfect for spontaneous crafting. And because of the low-tack quality of the tape, the projects can be redesigned when you want to create something new.

This book invites you to explore the endless possibilities of washi tape. I hope the projects will inspire you to discover your own uses for this versatile craft material. Now let's get started adding bold and colorful details to your décor, accessories, and packaging!

MATERIALS AND TOOLS

Many of the projects in this book require only a few basic supplies. Refer to this section when you have questions about the materials you'll need for your project.

ADHESIVES

Extra-Strength Glue (E6000)

E6000 is extra-strength liquid glue that will bond heavy materials to each other permanently. It's also waterproof.

Glue Dots

Glue Dots are small rounds of double-sided, dry but sticky adhesive that instantly create a bond. The benefit of Glue Dots is that you don't have to wait for them to dry. They work well for light materials such as paper.

BONE FOLDER

A bone folder is a plastic tool (traditionally made from bone) with a pointed edge used for creasing, scoring, and smoothing out paper. A Popsicle stick can be used in place of a bone folder.

CLEAR ACRYLIC PAINT

Clear acrylic paint is commonly used as a top coat to protect and seal an item, such as a decoupage project of layers of cutout paper pieces. Unlike other decoupage products, clear acrylic paint is water resistant when it dries, so I prefer it. Acrylic paint comes in various finishes, like gloss, matte, and satin.

CRAFT KNIFE

A craft knife is essential for cutting out areas that are hard to reach with scissors. It's important to have a craft knife with a sharp blade to make clean cuts.

CUTTING MAT

Use a cutting mat to protect your table when using scissors, craft knives, and even markers.

DECORATIVE HOLE PUNCHES

Decorative hole punches come in a variety of sizes and shapes. Just like a standard hole punch, they are used to punch out a shaped hole in a piece of paper or card stock.

PAPERS

Card Stock

Card stock is a heavyweight paper. It comes in varying weights, but I prefer to work with 110-lb/50-kg card stock (weight per a certain number of sheets). It's strong enough to construct a box, but it's thin enough to be used in a printer or copier.

Office Paper

Office paper is a lightweight paper, weighing 20 lb/9 kg (per a certain number of sheets). It's most commonly used for printing and copying.

Parchment Paper

Parchment paper is most commonly used in the kitchen these days, but it is also a useful craft paper. You can place pieces of tape on it for future use, and the tape will peel off easily when you're ready to use it.

RULER

A ruler is a straight edge used to measure and draw straight lines. Rulers come in different materials such as plastic (often transparent), wood, and metal. I prefer a metal ruler for its durability.

SCISSORS

Tape Scissors

A good pair of scissors for cutting tape is essential. You will need a sharp pair of scissors that makes precise cuts in the tape.

Decorative Scissors

Decorative scissors have blades with decorative edges. They will create cut edges of varying shapes, from hearts to scallops, and can be found at your local craft store.

WASHI TAPE

The building blocks of this book! Not all washi tape is the same quality. I've found that the Japanese washi tapes are thinner and more flexible. Tapes from other sources are usually not true washi and tend to be thicker, less flexible, and sometimes have a higher tack, making them more difficult to peel off, or a lower tack, meaning they don't stick as well. I prefer to use mt, a Japanese brand of washi tape. When picking out a tape, think about which characteristics (low tack vs. high tack, opaque vs. translucent, flexible vs. rigid) will be best suited to your project, and choose your tape accordingly. Also note that washi tape comes in several widths, so you'll want to choose a width that is appropriate for what you're making. Most of the projects in this book use the standard tape width: 5/8 in/16 mm. In a few projects, like the Greek Key Wall Border, I used a narrower tape, 1/4 in/6 mm. You can find washi tape at most craft stores, but for the mt brand you'll likely have to purchase it online. Two of my favorite places to purchase the tape are www .omiyage.ca and www.wishywashi.com.

TECHNIQUES

Some of the projects in this book use special techniques to help you create your projects with ease. Here's a review of these basic techniques.

ALIGNING WASHI TAPE ON PAPER

In this book, some projects require you to align the edges of the washi tape with a piece of paper. There are two ways to accomplish this with ease, either by cutting the tape away or cutting the paper away.

Cut Tape Away

Place washi tape on paper with the tape edges hanging off the paper's edges (see *Fig. 1*). Trim the tape ends with scissors so they are aligned with the paper's edges.

NOTE: *This method requires that you be precise when laying down the tape.*

Fig. 1

Cut Paper Away

Place washi tape on paper. With scissors, trim away the paper so the tape ends are aligned with the paper's edges (see *Figs. 2* and *3*).

Fig. 2

Fig. 3

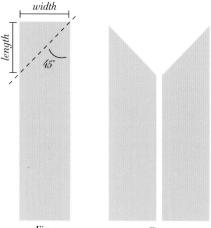

Fig. 1

Fig. 2

MITERED CORNER TECHNIQUE

To make your washi tape projects as seamless as possible, you'll want to miter the corners of your tape to create an almost invisible seam.

1. Measure the width of your washi tape. Use that measurement to make a mark from the top of your tape to that same measurement along the length of the tape. For example, if your tape is ⁵/₈ in/ 16 mm wide, measure down the length ⁵/₈ in/16 mm. Cut the tape along this 45-degree angle (see *Fig. 1*).

2. Cut a second piece of tape so the end is a mirror image of the end of the first piece of tape (see *Fig. 2*).

3. When you connect the ends of the two pieces of tape, you get a 90-degree mitered corner (see *Fig. 3*).

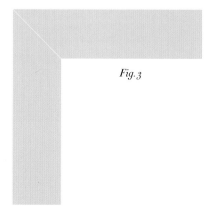

Fig. 3

NOTE: *Some projects may require a larger or smaller mitered angle. To achieve different mitered angles, you will need to cut the angle of your tape in step 1 less or more than 45 degrees.*

PARCHMENT PAPER CUTTING TECHNIQUE

Because washi tape is sticky, it can be hard to cut using only scissors. To make a more precise, straight cut, place your piece of tape onto a piece of parchment paper first. Then, using sharp scissors, cut through the tape and the parchment paper. You will get a clean cut, and you can keep the tape on the parchment paper until you're ready to use it.

SCORING

Scoring is a technique used to make a crisp fold or crease in a piece of paper. This technique is especially useful when you need to make multiple folds. It's also highly effective for folding large or heavyweight papers.

Hand-Scoring Office Paper and Card Stock Using a Bone Folder

Place the right side of your ruler about $1/16$ in/ 2 mm to the left of where you want to place a fold. With a bone folder, run it against the right side of the ruler while applying pressure into the paper to make an indentation. Your scoring line is now ready to fold.

Using a Craft Knife

Place the right side of your ruler flush with the line where you want to make a fold. With a craft knife, run it against the right side of the ruler, applying just enough pressure to make a shallow cut in the card stock or cardboard. Your scoring line is now ready to fold.

HOME DÉCOR

CATCHALL PLATE

····· **MAKES 1** ·····

Keep your loose change and keys organized with this striking catchall plate. Place it on an entryway credenza, a bedside table, or a desk for easy access.

SUPPLIES

Photocopier

1 piece of office paper, 8½ by 11 in/21.5 by 28 cm

Scissors

Pencil

1 piece of white card stock, 8½ by 11 in/21.5 by 28 cm

Ruler

Craft knife

Washi tape in 2 complementary colors (I used a chevron print tape)

Parchment paper

Foam paintbrush

Clear matte acrylic paint

1. On the piece of office paper, make a photocopy of the template in *Fig. 1*, enlarging it by 300 percent.

2. With the scissors, cut out the template on the solid lines.

3. With the pencil, trace the template onto the card stock, and cut it out along the pencil lines. On the card stock, draw in the dotted lines that form the base of the box.

4. With the ruler and craft knife, score gently along the dotted lines to make the card stock fold easily. Be careful not to cut through the card stock. Fold up the sides of the plate and then unfold.

5. Starting at the top card stock flap (see *Fig. 2*), place a piece of washi tape from side to side, with a little extra tape hanging over the edges. Repeat, placing another piece of washi tape just overlapping the first one, and so on, until the entire flap is covered with rows of tape. Trim the tape with scissors close to the edge of the card stock, as shown by the dotted lines in *Fig. 2*. Rotate the catchall plate 90 degrees to the right.

6. Repeat step 5 for the three other flaps until they are covered with washi tape. Flip the plate over.

7. Place the card stock flat on a piece of parchment paper slightly larger than the card stock plate.

{continued}

8. Starting at the top, lay a piece of washi tape on the card stock from side to side, with a little extra tape hanging off the edges. The card stock plate will be between the parchment paper and tape.

9. Place a second piece of washi tape parallel with the first so the edges just touch (see *Fig. 3*). Continue to cover the plate with washi tape until all of the card stock is covered.

10. With scissors, trim the excess tape on all the edges of the catchall plate.

11. Place a piece of the complementary washi tape on the edge of the top flap, with half of it hanging over (see *Fig. 4*). Fold that piece of tape over the edge of the flap and stick it to the back side. With scissors, trim any excess tape off the edges. Repeat this process for the remaining three flaps (see *Fig. 5*). Flip the plate over, back-side up.

12. Bring the two right corner flaps together. Place a piece of the complementary washi tape along the seam to tape the flaps together (see *Fig. 6*). Trim excess tape along the edges, as shown by the dotted lines in *Fig. 6*. Repeat this step for the three remaining corners.

13. With the foam paintbrush, cover the entire back side of the catchall plate with clear matte acrylic paint. Let dry for 1 hour.

14. Flip the catchall plate over, right-side up, and paint the entire top surface with the clear matte acrylic paint. Let dry for 1 hour.

CATCHALL PLATE, *Fig. 1*

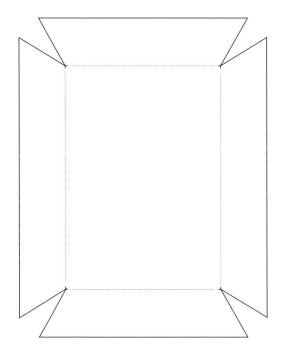

CATCHALL PLATE, *Figs. 2 through 6*

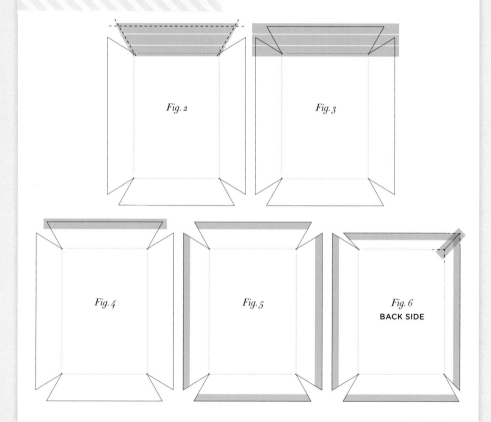

Fig. 2

Fig. 3

Fig. 4

Fig. 5

Fig. 6
BACK SIDE

FRAMED PIXEL HEART

····· **MAKES 1** ·····

Bring a little retro pop to any room with this bright heart pixel art. It's a great way to add a splash of color to any room. For a greater visual impact, make a set of three in complementary colors to hang on the wall together.

SUPPLIES

*1 piece of Bristol board,
11 by 14 in/28 by 35.5 cm*

Ruler

Pencil

Thin washi tape

Parchment paper

1. Starting at the left corner of the Bristol board, use the ruler to measure 5 in/12 cm up and 5¹/₂ in/14 cm to the right. Lightly mark that spot with the pencil. This is where you will place the center bottom square of washi tape for the heart.

2. Place a long strip of washi tape on a large piece of parchment paper. Cut the strip into squares. You will need a total of 68 squares.

3. Place your first square where you marked the Bristol board. Place seven squares in a vertical line above it, leaving about ¹/₁₆ in/2 mm of space between each square (see *Fig. 1*).

4. To the right of the first row, make a second column, as in *Fig. 1*.

5. Create four more columns to the right, until you have created the right half of the heart (see *Fig. 2*).

6. Now create the entire left side of the heart by placing squares down on the paper, one column at a time (see *Fig. 3*). I left out two squares as an accent on the left side of the heart. Feel free to improvise with your heart's design.

{continued}

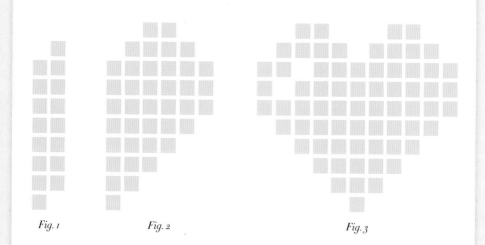

Fig. 1   *Fig. 2*   *Fig. 3*

DECORATED PHOTO MAT

····· **MAKES 1** ·····

You'll be surprised at how fast you can transform a standard mat for a picture frame and customize it for your home. With just a few well-placed strips of tape, you'll have a fresh and contemporary framed piece. Make these decorated mats for your wall or for gifts.

SUPPLIES

Pencil

Ruler

Mat frame for an 8-by-10-in/ 20-by-25-cm photo

Thin washi tape in 2 complementary colors and/ or different widths

Scissors

1. Starting at the left edge of the photo, use the ruler to measure 1 in/2.5 cm to the left of the photo and make a mark on the mat frame with the pencil. Use this mark to run a piece of washi tape vertically, parallel to the photo on the left side. The tape should extend from the top left edge to the bottom left edge of the mat frame.

2. Repeat step 1 for the right side of the mat frame. You will now have a piece of washi tape running parallel to each side of the photo.

3. Starting at the top edge of the photo, measure and mark the mat frame ³/₄ in/2 cm above the photo. Use this mark to run a piece of washi tape horizontally across, parallel to the top of the photo. The tape should extend all the way across the mat.

4. Repeat step 3 for the bottom of the photo. You will now have a piece of washi tape running parallel to the top and bottom of the photo.

5. Outside the previous four washi tape lines (farther from the photo), place a piece of tape of a complementary color parallel to each of the four previous tape lines, leaving about ¹/₄ in/6 mm between the tape lines.

GEMSTONE MIRROR

····· **MAKES 1** ·····

Refashion your mirror into a sparkly gem with this mirror border. All you need is a rectangular mirror and some tape to get started. Choose a color like silver for a subtle look or hot pink for a bold style. If your mirror has a beveled edge, like mine, work just inside the beveling.

SUPPLIES

Ruler

Dry-erase marker

Thin washi tape

Scissors

1. Starting at the top left corner of the mirror, with the ruler, measure from the left edge to the right 1½ in/4 cm and make a mark with the marker. Then measure 1½ in/4 cm down from the top and make a mark (see *Fig. 1*). Repeat for the remaining three corners. You now have made eight marks.

2. Place a piece of washi tape diagonally in the top left corner so it connects the marks in that corner. With scissors, trim the tape so it's flush with the edge of the mirror (see *Fig. 2*). Repeat for the three remaining corners.

3. On the left side of the mirror, place a vertical piece of washi tape so it connects the top and bottom pieces of washi tape. With scissors, trim the tape so it makes straight edges along the frame you are creating (see *Fig. 3*). Repeat for the right side.

4. Near the top, place a piece of washi tape on the mirror so it makes a horizontal line connecting the mark on the left vertical edge to the mark on the right vertical edge. With scissors, trim the tape so it's flush with the frame (see *Fig. 4*). Repeat at the bottom, making another horizontal line.

{continued}

5. At the top, place a piece of washi tape so it connects the two pieces of washi tape to the left and right, making the top edge of the frame. With scissors, trim the tape so it's flush with the frame (see *Fig. 5*). Repeat for the bottom, making the bottom edge of the frame. With scissors, trim the washi tape so it's flush with the frame.

6. On the left edge of the frame, place a piece of washi tape that connects the two pieces of washi tape at the top and bottom (see *Fig. 5*). With scissors, trim the tape so it's flush with the frame. Repeat for the right edge. Clean off any marks you can still see.

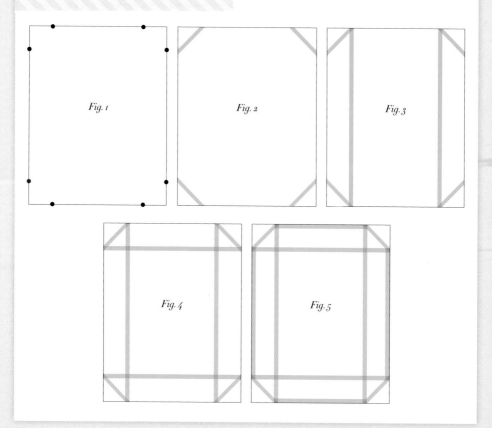

Fig. 1

Fig. 2

Fig. 3

Fig. 4

Fig. 5

BOOKSHELF WITH HARLEQUIN TRIM

····· **MAKES 1** ·····

This harlequin trim will give the humblest bookshelf a regal appearance.
All you need is a little tape to get started. Use this application for an entire
bookcase or a stand-alone shelf for a light decorative touch.

SUPPLIES

*Washi tape in
2 complementary colors*

Scissors

Parchment paper

Ruler

Pencil

1. Run a piece of washi tape across the entire front of your
bookshelf. With scissors, trim the ends of the tape for a
clean edge.

2. Place a piece of the complementary washi tape, about
12 in/30.5 cm long, on a slightly larger piece of parchment
paper. Measure the width of your tape (mine is 5/8 in/
16 mm), and mark the piece of tape in increments of that
measurement along the full length. Cut the washi tape to
make squares.

3. Peel off one square from the parchment paper and rotate
it 45 degrees so that it looks like a diamond. Place it at this
angle on the far left side of the washi-covered shelf front.

4. Peel off another square and place it beside the first diamond. Repeat, until the entire shelf front is covered with
a harlequin pattern.

FAUX HEADBOARD

····· **MAKES 1** ·····

Make a whimsical focal statement in your bedroom with this faux headboard. It's a great way to add a splash of color on the wall without the commitment of an actual headboard. Feel free to get creative and add finials or stripes to make it your own style.

SUPPLIES

Tape measure

Pencil

1 roll of washi tape

Scissors

Parchment paper

NOTE: *When creating the headboard, you'll want your bed to be slightly wider than the headboard. This project was designed for a standard twin-size bed. You may need to make adjustments for a bed that's a different size.*

1. Start with a clean wall and place your bed where you want it to be. Then move your bed forward a bit so you can mark on the wall. Find the center of your bed with the tape measure and lightly mark that spot on your wall with the pencil. Measure out 17½ in/44.5 cm from that point to the left and make a mark; measure the same distance from that center point to the right side and make a mark (shown by the two large black dots in *Fig. 1*). Those two marks are where the bases of the two outside bedposts will be. The bedpost bases will extend 2 in/5 cm down from the top of the bed to conceal the tape ends.

2. Now you will make the vertical lines for the left bedpost. From the dot for the base of the left bedpost (refer to the large black dots in *Fig. 1*), measure directly up 37 in/94 cm and lightly mark the wall with the pencil (see the large black dots in *Fig. 2*). Place a piece of washi tape from the bottom left dot to the top left dot on your wall.

{continued}

With scissors, trim the tape to make a straight edge, if needed. Working inside of the tape you just placed, add a second piece of washi tape that is parallel to the first piece, with a 1 in/2.5 cm gap between the two.

3. Repeat step 2 for the right bedpost. Finish off the bedposts with a 3 in/7.5 cm piece of washi tape placed horizontally on top of each of the two bedposts. To easily cut the washi tape, place a piece of tape on parchment paper, measure, and cut. Peel off the tape and place it on the wall.

4. Now you're going to make the top arches (see *Fig. 3*). Cut out all pieces of washi tape for the arches a little longer than the measurements shown in *Fig. 3*. Place the tape on the wall to form two parallel arches following the diagram, starting 4^{1}/$_{2}$ in/11.5 cm down from the tops of the bedposts. Your tape pieces will overlap a little. With scissors, trim the tape pieces so the edges line up together.

5. Now you will make the bottom edge of the headboard. Starting at the bottom inside of the bedposts (see *Fig. 3*), measure up 4 in/10 cm and mark with pencil lightly on the wall. Place a horizontal piece of washi tape from bedpost to bedpost. With scissors, trim the tape so the edges line up together.

6. Now you will make the vertical stripes of the headboard. Starting with the center stripes, use your tape measure and pencil to mark the top and bottom spots for placement of the two center pieces of washi tape, according to the measurements in *Fig. 3*. Place the washi tape on the wall and trim with scissors for clean edges.

7. According to the measurements in *Fig. 3*, measure and mark where the side vertical stripes of the headboard will be placed, between the center stripes and the bedposts. Place the washi tape on the wall to create the two vertical stripes on each side. Trim the tape with scissors for clean edges.

FAUX HEADBOARD, *Fig. 1*

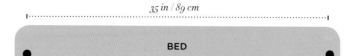

35 in / 89 cm

BED

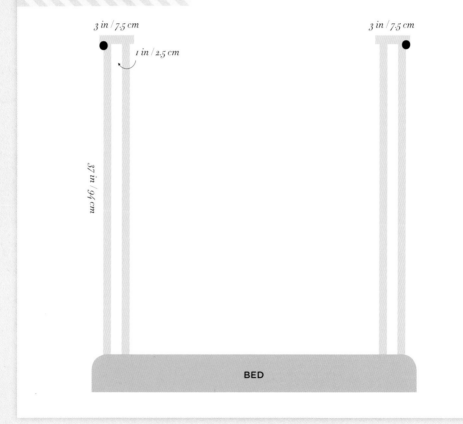

3 in / 7.5 cm

3 in / 7.5 cm

1 in / 2.5 cm

37 in / 94 cm

BED

FAUX HEADBOARD, *Fig. 3*

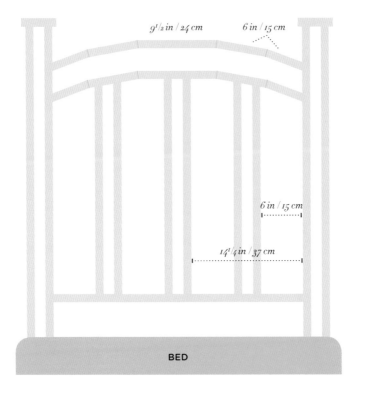

9$^1/_2$ in / 24 cm

6 in / 15 cm

6 in / 15 cm

14$^1/_4$ in / 37 cm

BED

GREEK KEY WALL BORDER

····· **MAKES 1** ·····

This ancient Greek key wall border is an elegant way to add color and detail to any room. Place it on one side of your room to create an accent wall or apply the border to the entire room. It works well at the top or at any height on your wall.

SUPPLIES

Parchment paper

1 roll of thin washi tape

Scissors

Pencil

Ruler

Eraser

NOTE: *For cutting washi tape, refer to the parchment paper cutting technique on page 15.*

1. Start with a clean wall. To make the top line of the border, starting where the wall and ceiling meet, place a piece of washi tape from the left side of the wall to the right side straight across. With the scissors, trim the tape. If you have crown molding, place the tape just below the crown molding instead.

2. With the pencil and ruler, place a mark at the left side of the wall 2¹/₄ in/5.5 cm down, where the bottom line will start. Make another mark at the same measurement on the right side of the wall. Then, to make the bottom line, place a second piece of washi tape from the left mark to the right mark, running parallel to your first piece of tape. Trim the tape (see *Fig. 1*).

3. Cut two pieces of washi tape with lengths of 1¹/₂ in/4 cm and 1¹/₄ in/3 cm. These two pieces will be joined to make an L shape.

{continued}

4. Place the two pieces of washi tape you just cut together using the mitered corner technique (see page 14) to create an upside-down L shape like in *Fig. 2*.

5. Now cut two more pieces of washi tape with lengths of 1⁵/₈ in/4 cm and 1¹/₄ in/3 cm and place to create a backward L (see *Fig. 3*).

6. Repeat steps 3 through 5 to complete the Greek key pattern (see *Fig. 4*), taking care to evenly space each L shape. Continue making the pattern until you have covered the entire length of the wall.

GREEK KEY WALL BORDER, *Figs. 1 through 4*

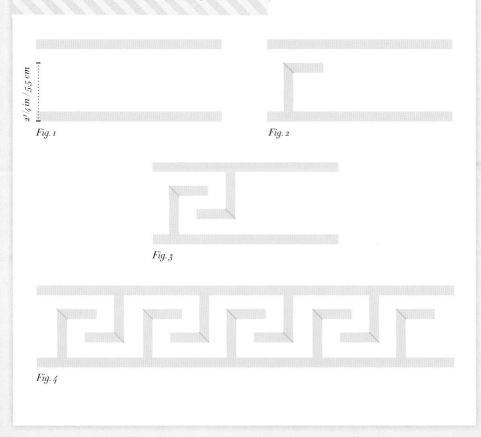

$2^{1}/4$ in / 5.5 cm

Fig. 1

Fig. 2

Fig. 3

Fig. 4

ORIGAMI CRANE WALL ART

····· **MAKES 1** ·····

Make a bold visual statement with this origami crane. For maximum effect, place the crane on an empty wall with little furniture. For a more subtle look, scale it down in size or use a color that creates a low contrast when against the wall.

SUPPLIES

Tape measure

Pencil

Ruler

Eraser

1 roll of washi tape

Thin washi tape

Scissors

1. Using your tape measure, pencil, and ruler, and creating 6-in/15-cm squares, very lightly draw a grid on your wall that is 6 squares high and 9 squares wide. If you want to make a smaller crane, make your wall grid squares smaller. You'll be using *Fig. 1* as a reference for where the crane fits within your squares.

2. You'll notice that the head of the crane is in the first square on the left and three squares down. So you'll place the head of your crane on the wall in the first square on the left and three squares down. The tip of the beak is in the bottom left corner of that square, so you'll begin by placing the beak in that section of the square on your wall. (Let the edges of the washi tape overlap; you'll trim them later.)

3. When placing washi tape on the wall to create the crane, make note of where the lines of the crane hit in the smaller grid squares of *Fig. 1*, and position the tape the same way in your larger squares on the wall. Do this to make the entire crane.

{ continued }

4. To make the center of the wings, run a piece of thin washi tape from the tip of the wings to the body.

5. Go back in with scissors and trim the tape where the edges overlap to make clean seams.

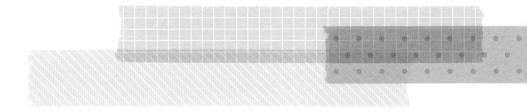

ORIGAMI CRANE WALL ART, *Fig. 1*

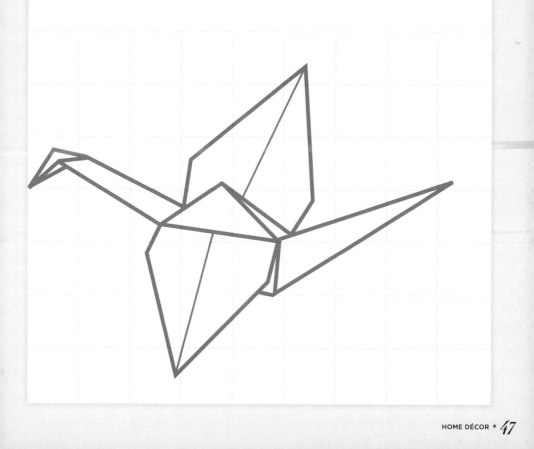

HOLIDAY GIFTS WALL ART

····· **MAKES 1** ·····

Deck the walls this holiday with these festive faux wrapped gifts. Place them so the presents look like they're sitting on a credenza or under the tree.

SUPPLIES

1 square piece of paper, 8 by 8 in/20 by 20 cm

Pencil

Ruler

Washi tape in 2 complementary colors

Scissors

Parchment paper

1. Place the paper square on the wall where you want to put the gift and trace around the edge of the paper square lightly with pencil.

2. Using the ruler, find the center of each side of the square and lightly mark with the pencil on the outside edge of the square.

3. To make a diagonal pattern with washi tape stripes to cover the entire square, start at the bottom left corner and work your way up to the top right corner, placing parallel stripes. Trim the ends of the washi tape stripes with scissors so they line up with the pencil edges of the box.

4. Using a washi tape of a complementary color, run a piece of tape down the center of the square vertically, and then run a piece of tape horizontally. Trim the edges of the tape so they line up with the box edges.

5. With four pieces of the complementary tape, make a box around the outer edge of the square. Line up the corners using the mitered corner technique (see page 14).

6. Cut ten small pieces of washi tape and place them on parchment paper in the shape of the bow in *Fig. 1*. Cut the bow on parchment paper to have rounded edges. Peel off the ten pieces of the bow one at a time and place them on the wall on top of the box.

{ continued }

TASSEL GARLAND

····· **MAKES 1** ·····

Add a festive touch to your party with a garland of these colorful tassels. Hang them all around or over a dessert table as a focal point. After the party, carefully wrap them up and store them for your next event.

SUPPLIES

Scissors

Washi tape in various complementary colors/ patterns

Ruler

String for tassel loops, and a piece long enough to hang all your tassels (use baker's twine, embroidery thread, or even fishing wire)

1. With the scissors, cut two pieces of washi tape about 4 in/ 10 cm long. Place the sticky sides together.

2. Cut the double-thick washi tape lengthwise into thin strips, stopping 1/2 in/12 mm from the top, to make fringe (see *Fig. 1*).

3. To make four more fringed pieces, repeat steps 1 and 2 four times. You will have five pieces of double-thick washi tape with fringe.

4. Stack the five pieces of washi tape on top of each other with the fringe facing down. Place a piece of 2-in-/5-cm-long string on the top in a loop (see *Fig. 2*).

5. At the top, roll the five pieces together tightly. Wrap a piece of coordinating-color washi tape around the top to secure (see *Figs. 2* and *3*).

6. Repeat steps 1 through 5 to create as many fringed tassels in as many colors as you'd like. String the tassels on a long piece of string to create a festive garland.

{continued}

TASSEL GARLAND, *Figs. 1 through 3*

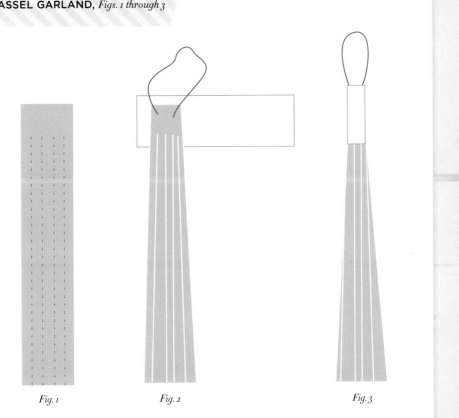

Fig. 1

Fig. 2

Fig. 3

DECORATIVE CURTAINS

····· **MAKES 1 CURTAIN PANEL** ·····

Add some graphic flair to your curtains—no sewing necessary! If you can place a piece of tape down, you can make this project. All you need is some tape and a sheer panel curtain to get started. You can find this style of curtain in the home section of most department stores. When you're ready to launder your curtains, you can quickly remove the tape and then replace it when they are clean.

SUPPLIES

Tape measure

Sheer curtain panel

Straight pins

Washi tape

Scissors

Iron

Tea towel (optional)

1. Using the tape measure, measure 3 in/7.5 cm up from the bottom of the sheer curtain panel on the left side. Place a pin on the curtain at that spot. Repeat on the right side of the panel.

2. Starting at the left side of the curtain panel, place down washi tape at the pinned spot. Run the tape across the panel to the pin on the right side. When you do this, keep the tape on the roll, and unroll it as you go. Cut the washi tape a little longer than the curtain width and fold it over to the back side at each edge. Remove the pins.

3. Now place washi tape along the bottom of the curtain. Starting at the left side of the panel, place the tape down and run it to the right side, just like you did in step 2.

4. With the iron set on the lowest heat, iron down the tape you just placed on the fabric. You can place the iron directly over the tape and iron it. I recommend testing the tape out on a small piece of fabric first. If the tape puckers or sticks to the iron, place a thin piece of fabric (such as a tea towel) over the tape before ironing. Ironing the tape onto the fabric will create a stronger bond.

TABLE SETTING VIGNETTE

····· **MAKES 1** ·····

With just a few humble supplies, you can convert any table with a festive place setting treatment. Use it for a casual meal with friends or for a large dinner party. Mix and match colors to create a setting that reflects your style.

SUPPLIES

White kraft paper, long and wide enough to cover your table plus overlap (optional)

Clear tape (optional)

Ruler

Pencil

Washi tape in 2 complementary colors

1. If you'd like to line your table, cover it now with white kraft paper and tape the edges underneath with clear tape.

2. Using the ruler, measure and mark with the pencil the center of the left and right ends of your table.

3. Run a piece of washi tape lengthwise along the center of the table from left to right. At each end, run the washi tape around the edge of the table and under; cut the ends, and tape them down with clear tape.

4. In the same manner, place a piece of washi tape of a complementary color 1 in/2.5 cm above the first piece. Then repeat with a piece of the complementary washi tape 1 in/ 2.5 cm below the first piece. You should now have three washi tape lines running along the center of the table.

5. Next, determine how many place settings you will have. For comfortable seating, a width of 24 to 30 in/61 to 76 cm per place setting is ideal. On one side of the table, measure the width of the place settings and mark with pencil. Make matching marks on the opposite side of the table.

6. For each pair of marks, run a piece of washi tape from one side of the table to the other to connect the marks. On each table edge, run the end of the washi tape under, cut, and stick down. You are now ready to set your festive table!

MOSAIC TILE COASTER

···· **MAKES 1** ····

Add a little old-world charm to your décor with these faux mosaic tile coasters. In this project, you'll be cutting out small triangles and squares from washi tape and sticking them to purchased tile coasters, to create your design. Use the coasters for cold lemonade or hot chocolate (just not as a hot plate).

SUPPLIES

Washi tape in 3 complementary colors

Parchment paper

Scissors

3½-in-/9-cm-square stone tile

Paintbrush

Clear gloss acrylic paint

4 felt pad stickers

1. Place a 6-in-/15-cm-long piece of washi tape on a piece of parchment paper slightly larger than the tape. With scissors, cut the tape in half lengthwise. Repeat with the remaining two tape colors.

2. Cut the tape into equal-size triangles and squares. My triangles have a length of ¼ in/6 mm and a width of ¼ in/6 mm, and my squares are ¼ in/6 mm by ¼ in/6 mm.

3. Pull off one washi tape triangle at a time from the parchment paper. To make the mosaic patterned border around the edge of the tile, place the triangles in alternating colors. To make the inner pattern, place the squares down to make two boxes, one inside the other.

4. When all the triangles and squares are placed, use the paintbrush to paint the entire tile with the clear gloss acrylic paint. Let dry for 20 minutes. Paint a second coat of acrylic paint on the tile. Let dry for 1 hour.

5. Add the felt pad stickers to the four bottom corners of the tile so it won't scratch your table.

SMOCKED PAPER LUMINARY

····· **MAKES 1** ·····

Create a warming ambiance in your room or at your next dinner party with this smocked paper luminary. Traditionally, smocking is a technique applied to fabric to create small gathers. This technique, when applied to paper, creates an unexpected texture for a lantern. Group a few lanterns together to make a statement or spread them out to create a warm glow.

SUPPLIES

1 piece of textured wrapping paper, 8 by 20½ in/20 by 52 cm

Bone folder (optional)

Ruler

Washi tape

Glue Dots

Battery-powered tea light

1. Using the ruler to measure, fold the piece of paper width-wise into ½-in/12-mm accordion folds. With a bone folder or other scoring tool, press down and rub along the folds to make them crisp.

2. Run a piece of washi tape across the center of your folded paper widthwise, taping every other fold together (see the black dots and dotted lines in *Fig. 1*). See *Fig. 2* for what the paper should look like with the tape in place. Leave a 2-in/5-cm tail of tape on one edge (see right side, *Fig. 2*).

3. Run another piece of washi tape along the top of the paper widthwise, ¼ in/6 mm from the top edge, taping every other fold together and leaving another 2-in/5-cm tail (see the orange dots and dotted lines in *Fig. 3*). Finally, run another piece of washi tape along the bottom of the paper, ½ in/12 mm from the edge (see *Fig. 4*).

4. From the back side, flatten out the paper surrounding the tape.

{continued}

5. With the taped side facing up, wrap the paper around to form a cylinder. Use Glue Dots to seal up the cylinder at the seam. Use the remaining tape tails at the edge to tape up the cylinder at the seam as well.

6. Place a battery-powered tea light inside your luminary at the base and watch it glow.

NOTE: *For safety, use only battery-operated tea lights for this project.*

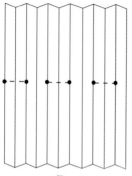

Fig. 1

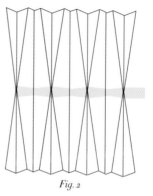

Fig. 2

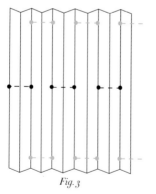

Fig. 3

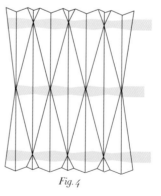

Fig. 4

ACCESSORIES

AND

EMBELLISHMENTS

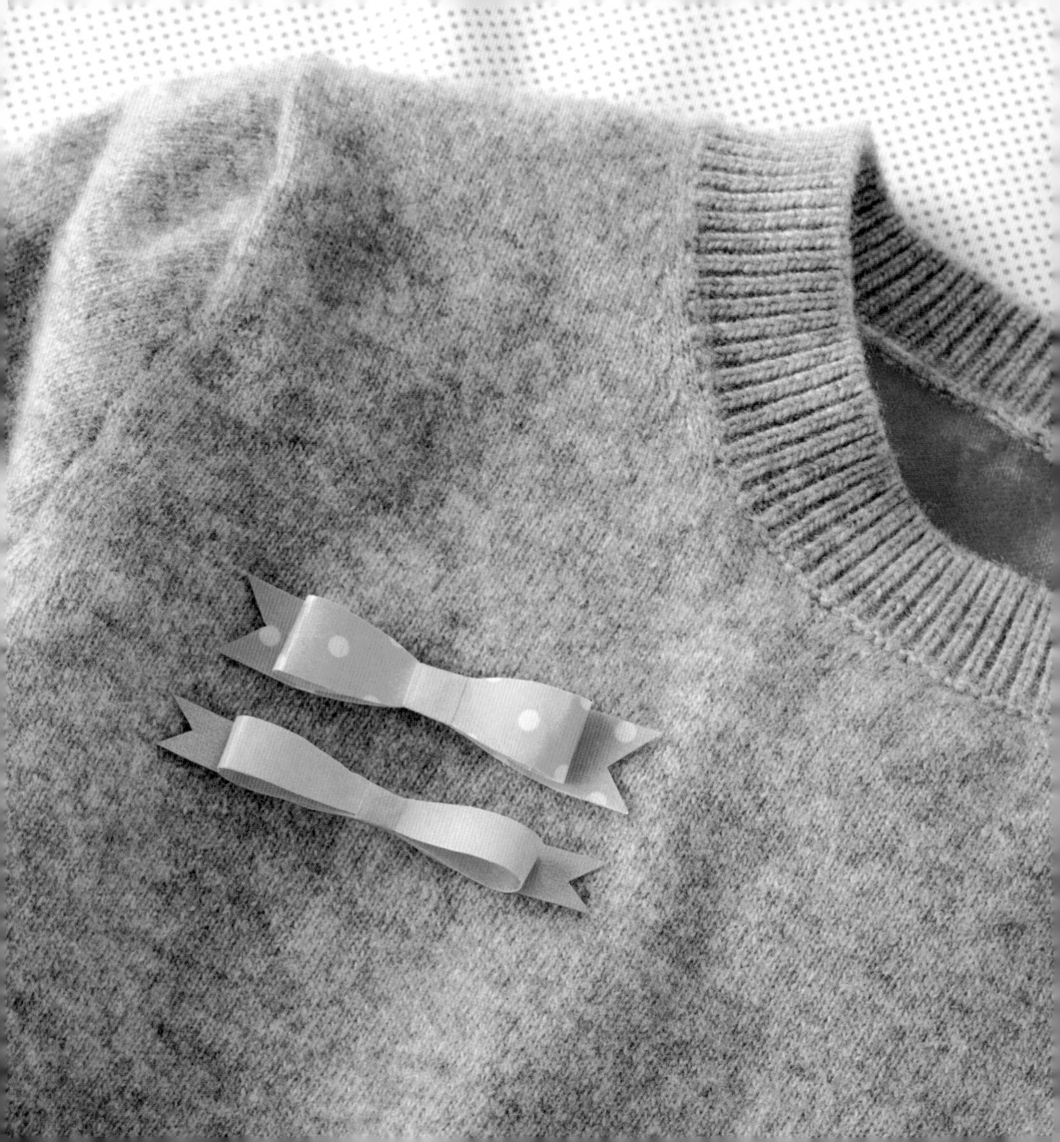

BOW BROOCH

These petite bows are perfect for adding pretty accents to your clothing. Mix and match colors to get different looks. You can also skip the pin back and tape the bows directly onto packages to make a sweet topper.

SUPPLIES

*Washi tape in
2 complementary colors*

Ruler

Scissors

Pin back

Extra-strength glue

I. Lay a piece of washi tape 4¹/4 in/10.5 cm long sticky-side up on a work surface.

2. Cut a piece of washi tape in the complementary color to the same 4¹/4-in/10.5-cm length. Place this piece on top of the first piece of tape, sticky-side down.

3. Form the double-thick tape strip into a loop, making sure that the ends overlap slightly (see *Fig. 1*).

4. Press the washi tape together in the center to create a bow shape (see *Fig. 2*). With scissors, cut through both layers of tape along the dotted lines in *Fig. 2* to shape the bow. The shape should now look like *Fig. 3*.

5. Cut a 1¹/2-in/4-cm piece of washi tape in the complementary color. Cut the tape lengthwise to create a thin strip of tape and set aside the rest for later. Wrap the strip around the center of the *Fig. 3* shape to form a bow. Set this part of the bow aside.

6. Next, make the piece that lies under the bow using the complementary color. Lay a 3-in-/7.5-cm-long piece of washi tape sticky-side up on the work surface.

7. Place a piece of washi tape of the same length on top of the first piece of tape, sticky-side down.

{continued}

8. With scissors, cut this double-thick washi tape strip using the dotted lines in *Fig. 4* as a guide.

9. Center the bow on top of the tape strip you just created.

10. Using the reserved piece of tape, wrap it around both the bow and the washi tape strip to hold them together. Cut the end of the tape so that the seam is hidden underneath the bow.

11. Adhere the bow to the pin back with extra-strength glue.

BOW BROOCH, *Figs. 1 through 4*

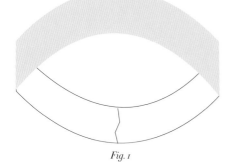

Fig. 1

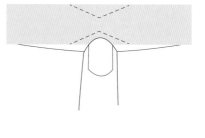

Fig. 2

Fig. 3

Fig. 4

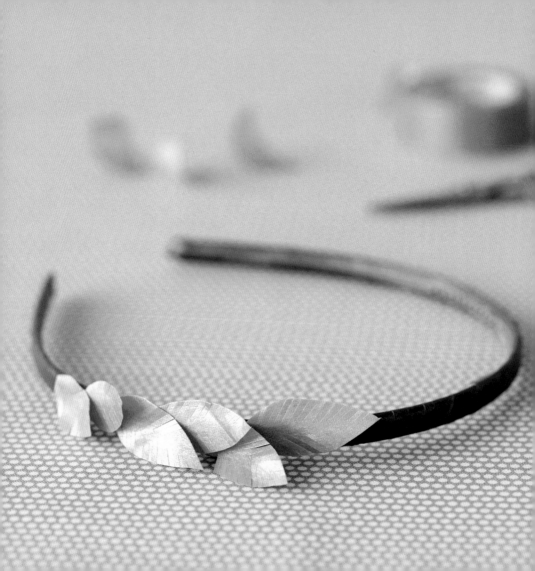

GOLD LEAF HEADBAND

····· MAKES 1 ·····

Transform a plastic headband into a chic hair accessory. You'll find that the gold washi tape takes on a faux leather look in this project. Make one headband or a few to mix and match with outfits.

SUPPLIES

Scissors

Washi tape in gold and a complementary color

Plastic headband (mine is $1/4$ in/6 mm thick, but use what you have on hand)

Paintbrush

Clear gloss acrylic paint

Extra-strength glue

1. With scissors, cut a piece of the complementary washi tape slightly longer than the length of the entire headband.

2. Starting at the left end of the headband, press the tape down on the headband and press with your fingers along to the right end, to cover the entire headband with the tape. Make sure to keep the tape centered along the headband at all times. The tape is wider than the headband, so there will be tape hanging off both sides (*Fig. 1*).

3. With scissors, cut slits in the washi tape on both sides that hang over the headband, according to dotted lines in *Fig. 2*. This will help you fold the tape underneath in sections to avoid wrinkling. Fold all tape sections to the underside and adhere (see *Fig 3*).

4. With a paintbrush, cover only the underside of the headband with one coat of clear gloss acrylic paint. This will keep the tape from peeling away. Let dry for 30 minutes while you work on the leaves.

{continued}

5. Place a 1¹/₂-in-/4-cm-long piece of gold washi tape sticky-side up on the work surface. Place another piece of gold washi tape of the same length directly on top of the first piece, sticky-side down. Make a total of six of these double-thick gold tape pieces.

6. With scissors, cut out a leaf shape that is 1¹/₂ in/4 cm long. At an angle, cut thin lines almost to the center of the leaf, using the dotted lines in *Fig. 4* as a guide, to give the illusion of leaf veins. Repeat, making a second leaf shape like the first one.

7. Then, make three leaves that are 1¹/₄ in/3 cm long, and one leaf that is ⁷/₈ in/2.5 cm long.

8. Dab some of the extra-strength glue on the bottom of one of the largest leaves. Attach the leaf to one side of the headband angled slightly to the left so the leaf sticks up slightly.

9. Now glue the other large leaf down so the top just overlaps the bottom half of the first leaf but angles out to the right.

10. Continue to glue the leaves onto the headband in descending size and alternating angled left, angled right, etc.

11. Let the glue dry for a full 24 hours before wearing the headband.

GOLD LEAF HEADBAND, *Figs. 1 through 4*

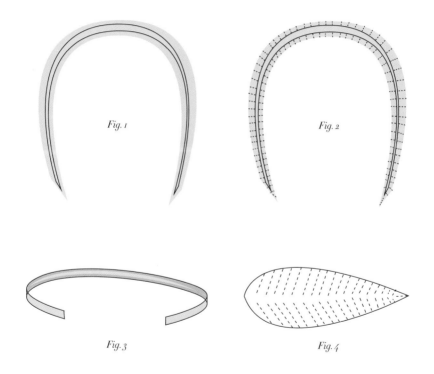

Fig. 1

Fig. 2

Fig. 3

Fig. 4

WASHI NAIL ART

···· **1 MANICURE** ····

Add a contemporary twist to your next manicure with this eye-catching nail art. Cover all of your nails or accent just a few nails with washi and use a complementary color for a statement. And unlike nail polish, tape comes in prints!

SUPPLIES

Washi tape in desired color/pattern

Scissors

Pencil

Parchment paper

Clear nail polish

1. Place a piece of washi tape directly on one of your fingernails so that it hangs off all sides.

2. Use the scissors to cut the tape off at the top of the nail, following your nail's shape.

3. With the pencil, draw along the sides and bottom of your nail bed, following the shape of your nail.

4. Pull the tape off your nail.

5. Place the tape on parchment paper. Cut along the pencil line to make the tape fit your nail.

6. Remove the tape from the parchment paper and place it back on your nail. If needed, trim the washi tape again for a perfect fit.

7. Repeat steps 1 through 6 for each nail.

8. Once your nails are covered with washi tape, apply two coats of clear nail polish, allowing the first coat to dry for about 1 minute before applying the second coat. Allow the second coat to dry for about 15 minutes.

HERRINGBONE CELL PHONE COVER

····· MAKES 1 ·····

Show off your unique style with this custom cell phone cover. Choose washi tape colors and prints that suit your taste. And when you feel like a new look, just peel the tape off and create something new!

SUPPLIES

Washi tape in 3 complementary colors/patterns

Cell phone cover

Pencil

Scissors

Craft knife

1. Place a piece of washi tape (color A in *Fig. 1*) down on the top of the cell phone cover at an angle.

2. With the pencil, mark the tape at the edge of the phone cover. Lift up the tape a little to trim it, cut off the excess tape, and then lay the tape back down on the phone cover.

3. Place a piece of washi tape (color B in *Fig. 2*) down on the top of the cell phone cover so the end lines up with the right side of washi tape color A (see dotted line, *Fig. 2*).

4. Using the method described in step 2, trim off the excess tape from the color B piece of washi tape. Feel around for the camera hole. With a craft knife, make an "x" on the tape over the hole. Fold the tape under the case so the camera hole is visible.

5. Place a piece of tape (color C in *Fig. 3*) down on the top of the phone cover so the bottom end lines up with the left side of the piece of washi tape color B (see dotted line, *Fig. 3*).

6. Place a piece of tape (color A in *Fig. 4*) on the phone cover, to continue the pattern. Continue to place pieces of washi tape in order (A, B, C, A, B, C) until the entire phone cover is covered with washi tape.

{continued}

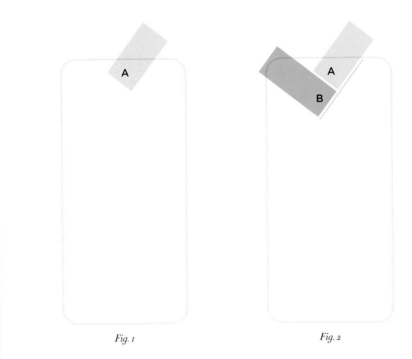

A

B

A

Fig. 1

Fig. 2

HERRINGBONE CELL PHONE COVER, *Figs. 3 and 4*

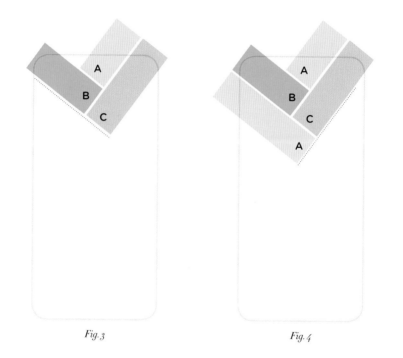

Fig. 3

Fig. 4

ARROWS CANVAS BAG

····· MAKES 1 ·····

Transform any basic canvas bag into a contemporary arrow print tote. Decorate just one side or both. And if you want to make a change in style, remove the tape and make something new!

SUPPLIES

Iron

*Canvas bag
(my bag is 13¹/₂ by 13¹/₂ in/
34 by 34 cm)*

Ruler

Scissors

*Thin washi tape in gold and
2 complementary colors*

Parchment paper

Tea towel (optional)

1. Iron the canvas bag so you're starting with a smooth fabric surface.

2. Using the ruler and scissors, measure and cut three 10-in/ 25-cm strips of gold washi tape and place them on the parchment paper.

3. Starting 3 in/7.5 cm up from the bottom left corner of the bag, place one of the gold washi tape strips on the bag horizontally.

4. On the right side of the bag, place a second horizontal gold washi tape strip 3 in/7.5 cm above the first piece of tape.

5. On the top left side of the bag, place a third horizontal strip of gold washi tape 3 in/7.5 cm above the second piece of tape.

6. Measure and cut six 1¹/₂-in/4-cm gold washi tape strips for the points of the three arrows. Place two of those strips on the end of each gold strip to make the arrow point (see *Fig. 1*) using the mitered corner technique (see page 14).

{continued}

7. Measure and cut eight 1¼-in/3-cm strips of washi tape in one of the complementary colors for the arrow feathers. Place four tape pieces each on the back end of the top and bottom arrows (see *Fig. 2*), using the mitered corner technique to angle the pieces.

8. Measure and cut four 1¼ in/3 cm strips of tape in the other complementary color. Place those four tape strips on the back end of the middle arrow (see *Fig. 2*), again angling the strips.

9. With your iron on the lowest heat setting, press the tape onto the fabric to ensure a strong bond between the two materials. Take care to not burn the tape. You might want to test out ironing a small piece of tape first. If the tape puckers, place a thin piece of fabric (like a tea towel) between the tape and the iron.

ARROWS CANVAS BAG, *Figs. 1 and 2*

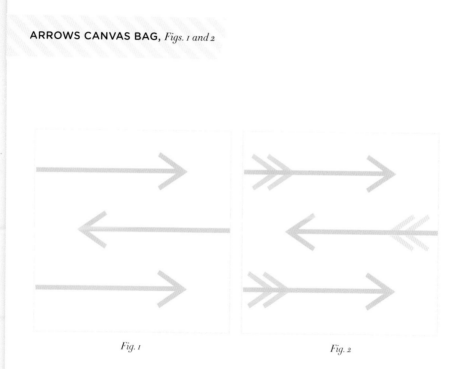

Fig. 1

Fig. 2

BEAUTIFIED BASKET

····· **MAKES 1** ·····

With just a little well-placed washi tape, you can transform a basket into an eye-catching contemporary accessory. Decorate the top of the basket or the entire piece to suit your taste.

SUPPLIES

Tape measure

Wood basket

Scissors

Washi tape

Toothpick

1. Using the tape measure, measure the length of one exposed section of a horizontal wood strip on your basket.

2. Cut a piece of washi tape slightly longer than the exposed section.

3. Place the piece of washi tape centered on that section of the horizontal wood strip. With a toothpick, tuck both ends of tape under the vertical strips of the basket and press down to adhere.

4. Repeat, for all parts of the basket you want to decorate.

5. For my basket, I also placed a continuous piece of tape around the top since it had a large border. This is optional.

EMBELLISHED BIRTHDAY CANDLE

····· MAKES 1 ·····

Brighten up the simplest of birthday cakes with a revamped candle number. Make them in a neon pink with gold trim to stand out or use a fun print to go with the theme. These directions may vary a little depending on what number you are decorating. Caution: Leave room between the wick and the washi tape. Never leave a lit candle unattended.

SUPPLIES

Number candle

Craft knife

Scissors

*Washi tape in
2 complementary colors*

Parchment paper

Pencil

1. If your number candle has decorative dots on it, scrape them off with a craft knife. If you don't do this, they will show through the tape.

2. To cover the raised edge of the number, choose one side of the candle to start with. With scissors, cut a piece of washi tape about the same length as that side and place it on parchment paper. Cut the tape in half lengthwise.

3. Peel one strip of the washi tape off the parchment paper and place on the raised edge of the number. Press the tape down so it covers both sides of the raised edge.

4. Repeat steps 2 and 3 until the entire raised edge of the number is covered with washi tape.

5. Place a piece of washi tape in a complementary color at the top of the inside of the raised edges. Push the tape down with your finger and trace the inside with a pencil. Pull the tape off the candle.

{ continued }

6. Place that piece of washi tape on parchment paper and use scissors to cut around the marks you just made. Peel the tape off the parchment paper and place it back on the candle.

7. Repeat steps 5 and 6 until the entire inside of the candle is covered.

8. Turn the candle over and repeat steps 2 through 7 to cover that side with washi tape.

9. Now you're going to cover the sides of your candle. Start with the top of the candle. Make sure to place the tape at least 1/4 in/6 mm away from the wick on each side. (The tape should be far enough from the wick that it doesn't catch fire.) Center the tape on top of the candle.

10. With scissors, cut the tape on the sides according to the dotted lines in *Fig. 1* (you can see the candle wick in the center). Fold down any excess tape that you just cut on the sides of the candle.

11. Repeat steps 9 and 10 for each side of the candle.

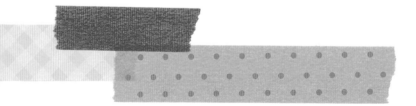

EMBELLISHED BIRTHDAY CANDLE, *Fig. 1*

Fig. 1

PARTY HAT MAGNETS

····· **MAKES 1** ·····

Make every photo a party with these fun magnets. Use them to showcase friends and family on a fridge, bulletin board, or even a locker. Create them in various sizes to get the perfect fit for each picture.

SUPPLIES

Pencil

1 magnet sheet, 3 by 4 in/ 7.5 by 10 cm

Scissors

Washi tape in 2 complementary colors

Parchment paper

Glue Dot

Mini pom-pom

1. Draw a party hat shape on the magnet sheet and cut it out with scissors (my hat is 2^1/$_2$ in/6 cm tall with a 2 in/ 5 cm base).

2. Place lengths of both colors of washi tape onto parchment paper and cut into narrow strips (about ^{1}/$_8$ in/3 mm wide).

3. Peel off a strip of washi tape in one color and place it at the bottom left corner of the hat, slanted down to the right.

4. Peel off a strip of washi tape in the complementary color and place it above the first piece of tape. Continue to add strips in alternating colors up to the top of the hat until the entire hat is covered in stripes. Fold the tape ends to the back of the magnet, trimming if necessary.

5. Place the Glue Dot at the top of the hat and stick on the mini pom-pom.

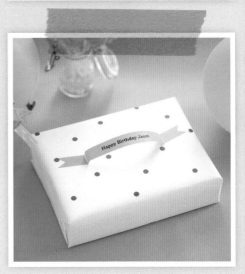

STATIONERY

=== AND ===

PACKAGING

TRANSFERRED PHOTO CARD

····· **MAKES 1** ·····

Personalize stationery with this unique photo card. Transferring an image with washi is as simple as printing on an inkjet printer and placing the washi tape down. When the cards are done, they're perfect for any occasion from birthdays to graduation to Valentine's Day.

SUPPLIES

Inkjet printer

2 pieces of card stock, one 8¹/₂ by 11 in/21.5 by 28 cm and a second one 6¹/₂ by 10 in/16.5 by 25 cm

Washi tape

Scissors (optional)

1. With an inkjet printer, print a 3-by-3-in/7.5-by-7.5-cm black-and-white high-contrast image on the 8¹/₂-by-11-in/21.5-by-28-cm piece of card stock.

2. Place a piece of washi tape over the top of the image width-wise. The tape should be slightly longer than the width of the image.

3. Place another piece of washi tape on the image directly under the first piece so the edges touch. Repeat, until your image is completely covered with tape.

4. Fold the 6¹/₂-by-10-in/16.5-by-25-cm piece of card stock in half to make a 6¹/₂-by-5 in/16.5-by-12-cm card.

5. Decide where you want the top of your image to be on your card. Peel off the top piece of washi tape from the image and place it on the card. When you peel off the tape, the ink from your image will have transferred to the tape, and the image will show through the sheer tape.

6. Continue to pull each piece of tape off the printed image and place it on your card in descending order. You can "crop" your image by cutting the edges evenly or leave them varied for a more handmade feel.

EMBELLISHED ENVELOPE

····· **MAKES 1** ·····

Surprise your friends with these delightful lined envelopes. Mix and match colors and prints to coordinate with your cards or make a special set for invitations to a party.

SUPPLIES

Envelope

Washi tape in
2 complementary colors

Scissors

Parchment paper

Pencil

1. With the envelope closed, place two pieces of washi tape overlapping the bottom edge of the top flap (see *Fig. 1*). Trim the tape with scissors along the dotted lines.

2. Place a 5-in-/12-cm-long piece of tape on parchment paper. Cut the tape in half lengthwise to make a thin strip of tape.

3. Open up the envelope and place a strip of washi tape on both bottom flap seams of the envelope (see *Fig. 2*). Trim the tape along the edges of the envelope.

4. Place parchment paper on top of the envelope, and with the pencil, trace the area of the exposed inside of the envelope but not including the glue edge (see *Fig. 3*). Remove the parchment paper, and you will see a shape that looks like the one in *Fig. 4*.

5. Flip the parchment paper over, and you'll still be able to see your pencil line. On this side of the parchment paper, starting at the top of your drawing, place a piece of washi tape of a complementary color on the top point of your shape. It's okay if it overlaps the edges; you'll trim it later.

{ continued }

6. Place a second piece of washi tape edge to edge below the first piece of tape, matching up the tape pattern if needed. Continue to do this until the entire shape is covered with washi tape.

7. Flip over the parchment paper. Using the line you drew as a template, cut the traced outline out with scissors.

8. Peel off the washi tape and position it on the inside of your envelope (see *Fig. 5*). The tape may come off in one big piece. If not, peel one tape piece off at a time and reposition it on the inside of the envelope.

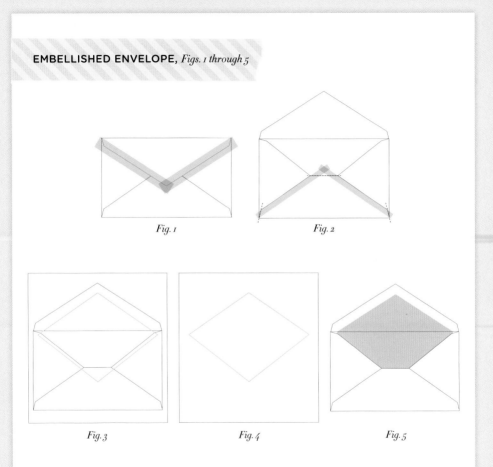

Fig. 1

Fig. 2

Fig. 3

Fig. 4

Fig. 5

CUSTOM JOURNAL COVER

····· **MAKES 1** ·····

Dress up any journal with these washi tape stickers. You can make them in just about any shape and color to suit your style. If you're having too much fun decorating, when you're done with the cover, open up the journal and add some accents to the interior pages.

SUPPLIES

Washi tape in 2 to 3 complementary colors

Parchment paper

Decorative hole punch smaller than the width of the washi tape (available in various hole shapes)

Paper-covered journal for decorating

Sponge brush

Clear gloss acrylic paint

1. Place a long piece of each color of washi tape, sticky-side down, on the parchment paper.

2. Use the decorative hole punch to cut out shapes. If you'd like different shapes, use a variety of punches. The number of shapes needed will depend on the size of the journal and the type of shapes you make.

3. Lay down the washi tape shapes on the journal cover to decide your desired final array.

4. Peel the washi tape shapes off the parchment paper and stick them on the journal.

5. With the sponge brush, paint a layer of the clear gloss acrylic paint over the journal's entire front surface. Let dry for 30 minutes.

MINI NOTEBOOK

····· **MAKES 1** ·····

This pint-size notebook is the perfect journal to keep in your handbag for when you need to jot down a note. Make a few in different styles so you'll always have one on hand.

SUPPLIES

1 piece of white card stock, 3¹/₂ by 6 in/9 by 15 cm

Washi tape in 2 complementary colors

Scissors

Ruler

Pencil

Decorative hole punch (my hole punch measures 1¹/₂ by 1 in/4 by 2.5 cm)

5 pieces of office paper, 3¹/₂ by 6 in/9 by 15 cm

Stapler

Pen

1. To make the cover of the mini notebook, starting at the top left corner of the card stock, place a piece of washi tape horizontally across to the right corner.

2. Line up a second piece of tape directly below the first piece and lay it across the card stock. Repeat, covering the card stock with washi tape strips until the entire piece is covered with tape. With scissors, trim excess tape ends if needed.

3. Flip the card stock over. From the left side, use the ruler to measure over 1¹/₂ in/4 cm to the right and mark at the top with pencil.

4. Center the decorative hole punch ¹/₂ in/12 mm down from the mark you just made and punch out a shape to make the decorative window on the front of the notebook.

5. Stack the five pieces of office paper on top of the card stock so the edges match up. Fold the stack of paper in half and then unfold.

6. Staple the paper pieces and card stock together on the center fold at the top and bottom (total of two staples).

{continued}

7. Flip the book over, lay it flat (unfolded), and place a strip of washi tape down the center of the card stock, which will be the spine of your notebook. Trim off any excess tape ends.

8. Fold the entire book in half, so the cover faces out.

9. With the pen, write a word or two on the first page of the notebook, so the words show through the punched window.

TRIANGLE FAVOR

Impress your friends with these triangle favors that are deceptively simple to make. Use them for party favors or to wrap a small gift such as a pair of earrings.

SUPPLIES

1 section of office paper, 7 1/2 by 3 in/19 by 7.5 cm

Washi tape

Scissors

I. Fold both sides of the paper along the dotted lines shown in the diagram so they meet in the center (see *Figs. 1* and *2*). Secure the seam with a piece of washi tape that is longer than the height of the paper. To hide the ends of the tape, fold them under the top layer of paper.

2. Place a piece of washi tape at the bottom of your favor perpendicular to the first piece of tape, with half of it hanging off the bottom edge. Fold that half onto the other side to seal the favor at the bottom.

3. Press in the sides of the favor to open the top (see *Fig. 3*). The favor will form a bag, with a top edge that is perpendicular to the sealed bottom edge. Place goodies inside the bag and seal the top closed with a piece of washi tape so your favor looks like *Fig. 4*. Trim the tape with scissors if needed. Embellish with more washi tape if you like.

{continued}

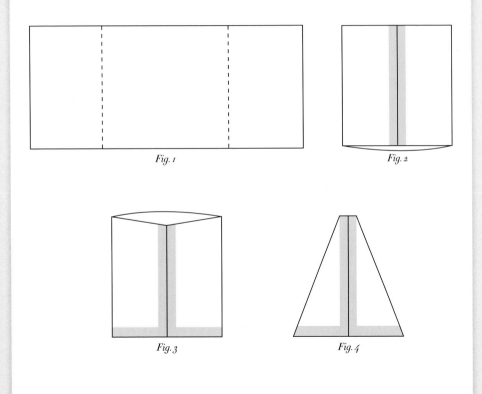

Fig. 1

Fig. 2

Fig. 3

Fig. 4

WASHI-TRIMMED CELLOPHANE BAG

····· **MAKES 1** ·····

Add an extra decorative element to your parties with these festive
cellophane favors. Fill them with your favorite treats for guests to take
home, make them part of the table setting, or place them in a basket
to hand out at the end of your event.

SUPPLIES

*Cellophane bag
(my bag is 4 by 3 in/
10 by 7.5 cm)*

Scissors

Washi tape

1. Trim the top of the cellophane bag with scissors to make
it the size you want.

2. Place a piece of washi tape across the bottom of the bag.
Flip the bag over and place a second piece of tape on the
bottom of the other side. Trim the ends of the washi tape,
being careful not to cut the bag.

3. Fill the cellophane bag with favors.

4. To seal the bag, place a piece of washi tape along the top
of the bag, leaving half of it extending beyond the top.
Flip the bag over and place a piece of tape on the other
piece of tape, sticky-side down, so they seal the bag shut.
Carefully trim off the ends of the excess washi tape.

WAX PAPER FOOD WRAP

····· **MAKES 1** ·····

Make homemade baked treats look extra tempting with this pretty food wrap. Customize the colors to complement the occasion, whether it's for a birthday party or bridal shower.

SUPPLIES

2 pieces of wax paper large enough to wrap your item

Ruler

Pencil

Washi tape

Tea towel or piece of cloth

Iron

Scissors

Baker's twine

1. Tear two pieces of wax paper from the roll so they are square. Don't worry about the ripped edges—you'll trim them in a later step.

2. Starting at the top left corner of one wax paper square, use the ruler to measure 1 in/2.5 cm down from the top and make a mark with the pencil. Repeat for the top right corner. Place a piece of washi tape across from one mark to the other.

3. Below the first piece of washi tape, continue to place pieces of tape across the wax paper, making a stripe pattern with a 1/2-in/12-mm gap between each piece of tape.

4. Place the second piece of wax paper on top of the first piece so it's covering the entire piece. It's okay if it's not exactly the same size.

5. Place the tea towel on top of the wax paper to protect your iron from the wax paper. With your iron set to medium-low heat, move the iron around slowly and iron the two sheets of wax paper together until they are completely sealed, about 30 seconds.

6. Use the scissors to trim the bonded washi-striped wax paper to the size you want for wrapping your item. Wrap up your pretty package with the baker's twine.

CUPCAKE TOPPER

····· **MAKES 1** ·····

Make any treat festive with these cute cupcake toppers. They're simple to make and only require a few supplies. Make them in different colors and prints to coordinate with your event.

SUPPLIES

2 pieces of thin washi tape, 3 in/7.5 cm long

2 toothpicks (ones with tooled tops can be found at most Asian grocery stores)

Fine-point marker

1. Lay one piece of washi tape sticky-side up on a work surface.

2. Place the toothpicks on top of the tape, about 2 in/5 cm apart and angled with the bottom points facing in.

3. Place the second piece of washi tape directly on top of the first piece of tape, sticky-side down, and press to seal the toothpicks inside.

4. Cut a V shape out of each end of the double-sided tape.

5. Write your message on the center of the tape with the marker. Let dry for 2 minutes.

PRETTY TWIST TIE

····· **MAKES 1** ·····

Who said twist ties have to be ordinary? Make your own with washi tape and revamp a basic bag into a decorative package with just a few twists. These fun twist ties can have bold prints and colors for all your packaging needs.

SUPPLIES

Washi tape

Scissors

Wire cutters

24-gauge wire

Decorative scissors (optional)

1. Cut two pieces of washi tape to the length you would like your twist tie to be (5 in/12 cm is a good length).

2. With the wire cutters, cut a piece of wire 1/2 in/12 mm shorter than the length of washi tape.

3. Center the piece of wire lengthwise on the sticky side of one piece of your washi tape.

4. Place the second piece of washi tape directly on top of the wire and tape, sticky-side down.

5. Seal by rubbing your finger across the tape. Trim the ends of the double-thick washi tape twist tie to make them even, or cut a V shape out of each end.

6. Repeat steps 1 through 5, to make as many twist ties as you wish.

NOTE: *For even-more-detailed twist ties, trim all the edges of the tape with decorative scissors.*

WINDOW GIFT BAG

····· **MAKES 1** ·····

Wrap up gifts in a pinch with this charming window bag. The washi tape–framed window gives your recipient a sneak peek at what they're receiving, so you can add sweet treats or show a cute stuffed animal peeking out. For this project, you'll be making your own bag using the provided template, enlarged on a copier.

SUPPLIES

1 sheet of scrapbook paper, 12 by 12 in/30.5 by 30.5 cm

Pencil

Eraser

Ruler

Scissors

Craft knife

Bone folder (optional)

Clear tape

1 piece of cellophane, 4 by 3 in/10 by 7.5 cm

Washi tape

Parchment paper

Decorative scissors

Glue Dots

1. Make a copy of the template in *Fig. 1*, enlarging it by 250 percent.

2. On the back of the sheet of scrapbook paper, trace the template with a pencil. Mark the folds (dotted lines) and the window. Cut out the template on the solid outside line.

3. With the craft knife, cut out the rectangle window (see *Fig. 1*).

4. Fold the paper on all dotted lines to make the bag shape. If you have a bone folder, use it as a scoring tool along the dotted lines to make the folding process easier. Then open the gift bag up and lay it on a work surface wrong-side up.

5. With the clear tape, tape the piece of cellophane over the window on the inside of the bag. Flip the bag over, right-side up. Set the bag aside.

6. With scissors, cut two pieces of washi tape 3⅝ in/9 cm long and two pieces 2¾ in/7 cm long. Place the four tape pieces on the parchment paper.

7. Using the decorative scissors, for all four tape strips, cut one side of the tape to make a scalloped edge. The width of your tape should now be just a little over ¼ in/6 mm.

{continued}

8. On the front of the bag, place the four washi tape strips to cover the edges of the window, making sure the tape overlaps onto both the paper and the cellophane window. Line up the tape at the corners using the mitered corner technique (see page 14).

9. Refold the paper into a bag shape. With Glue Dots, adhere the tab along the side of the bag under the 4-in/10-cm panel on the back side.

10. With Glue Dots, adhere the tabs at the bottom of the bag.

11. To close the bag, fold the top over or simply pinch the bag front and back together and seal with a piece of washi tape.

WINDOW GIFT BAG, *Fig. 1*

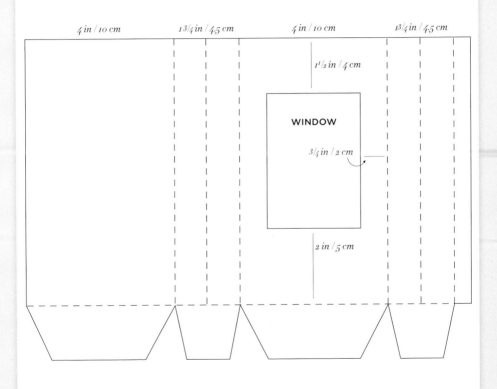

4 in / 10 cm   1¾ in / 4.5 cm   4 in / 10 cm   1¾ in / 4.5 cm

1½ in / 4 cm

WINDOW

¾ in / 2 cm

2 in / 5 cm

GIFT BOX WITH POCKET

····· **MAKES 1** ·····

Besides adding a cute touch to your package, this pocket doubles as a card holder—an embellishment with a practical function! Mix and match tape colors and prints to add your personal touch.

SUPPLIES

Washi tape in 2 complementary colors

Wrapped gift box (I used a box 14 by 9¹/₂ in/ 35.5 by 24 cm)

Scissors

1 sheet of office paper, 8¹/₂ by 11 in/21.5 by 28 cm

Parchment paper

Pencil

1. Place a piece of washi tape vertically on the left side of your gift box. Let the tape ends run over the edges.

2. Place a piece of washi tape horizontally on your gift box near the top of the box so the tape ends run over the edges.

3. Cut a piece of office paper in your desired pocket shape (see *Fig. 1*). My pocket is 3 by 4 in/7.5 by 10 cm. Place this paper pocket template on parchment paper.

4. Starting at the left side of the pocket shape, place a piece of the first color of tape at the top of the pocket, so only ¹/₄ in/6 mm covers the office-paper pocket, and there is extra tape on both the left and right sides.

5. With your washi tape of a complementary color, place a piece right under the first piece of tape, running it across the width of the pocket with tape hanging off the edges of the office-paper pocket and onto the parchment paper.

6. Repeat step 5, moving down on the pocket, until the entire pocket is covered with tape.

{continued}

7. At the top of the pocket, cut off any excess tape with scissors.

8. For the rest of the pocket, cut around the sides, leaving a ¼-in/6-mm allowance around the office paper where you see the dotted lines in *Fig. 1*. This will allow you to stick your pocket to the gift box.

9. Peel the entire washi tape pocket off the parchment paper and position the pocket where the strips of the tape "ribbon" intersect.

GIFT BOX WITH POCKET, *Fig. 1*

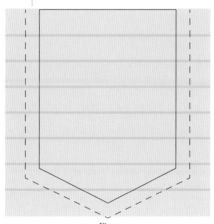

¹/₄ in / 6 mm

Fig. 1

GIFT TAG BANNER

····· **MAKES 1** ·····

Add a little whimsy to your packages with this festive gift tag banner. It's a fun alternative to the classic gift tag, perfect for writing small notes in style.

SUPPLIES

1 piece of washi tape, 6 1/2 in/16.5 cm

1 section of white office paper, 4 by 1 in/ 10 by 2.5 cm

Scissors

Parchment paper

Fine-point marker

1. Lay the piece of washi tape on the section of office paper, centering it so an equal amount of extra tape hangs over both sides (see *Fig. 1*).

2. Trim the excess paper off above and below the washi tape so there's no paper visible. You now have a strip of tape and only the ends are sticky.

3. Place the piece of washi tape on the parchment paper and cut a V shape out of each end.

4. Write a message on the center of the tape with the marker. Let dry for 2 minutes.

5. Peel the finished gift tag off the parchment paper and position it on the package so it arches up.

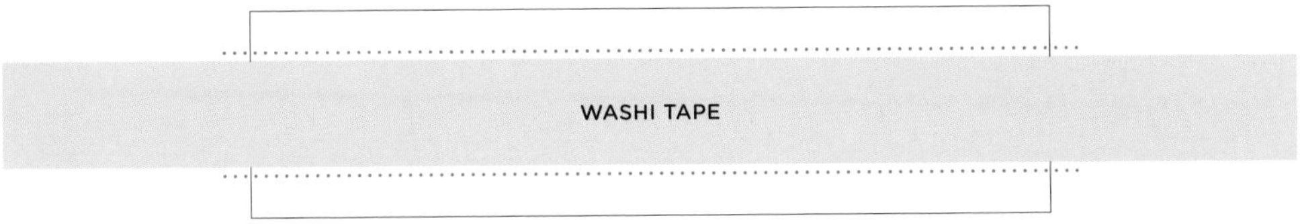

WASHI TAPE

Fig. 1

FLOWER BOUQUET WRAP

····· **MAKES 1** ·····

Show you care with custom packaging on your flower bouquet. This wrap is easy to make and can be personalized for any occasion. Choose your colors to complement the bouquet.

SUPPLIES

1 sheet of brown kraft paper, 14 by 14 in/35.5 by 35.5 cm (size of paper may vary depending on how large a bouquet you're wrapping)

Ruler

Pencil

Washi tape in 2 complementary colors

Scissors

Pen

1. From the top left corner of your kraft paper, use the ruler to measure 1¼ in/3 cm down from the top edge and mark with the pencil. Repeat for the top right corner. Place a piece of washi tape across from one mark to the other.

2. Repeat, making stripes with the same color washi tape, moving down the sheet of kraft paper. I spaced my tape stripes 1 in/2.5 cm apart, but feel free to vary the design to your liking. If needed, trim excess tape with the scissors.

3. Flip the sheet of kraft paper over and turn it to the left 45 degrees to make a diamond shape. Place your flower bouquet in the center of the paper, poking up out of the top slightly.

4. Fold the right corner to the left so it just covers the flowers.

5. Fold the left corner over the right. Tape down that corner with washi tape to secure. You've now wrapped your bouquet.

6. Write a message to the recipient or the person's name on a piece of the complementary washi tape. Place it on the top center of the wrap.

HAVE
FUN!